FORGET THE
ELEPHANTS, WATCH
OUT FOR THE FLEAS

JUSTIN HERALD

FORGET THE ELEPHANTS, WATCH OUT FOR THE FLEAS

It's the small issues that create the big problems

ALLEN&UNWIN

Copyright © Justin Herald 2009

All rights reserved. No part of this book may be reproduced or transmitted in any form or by any means, electronic or mechanical, including photocopying, recording or by any information storage and retrieval system, without prior permission in writing from the publisher. The *Australian Copyright Act 1968* (the Act) allows a maximum of one chapter or 10 per cent of this book, whichever is the greater, to be photocopied by any educational institution for its educational purposes provided that the educational institution (or body that administers it) has given a remuneration notice to Copyright Agency Limited (CAL) under the Act.

Allen & Unwin
83 Alexander Street
Crows Nest NSW 2065
Australia
Phone: (61 2) 8425 0100
Fax: (61 2) 9906 2218
Email: info@allenandunwin.com
Web: www.allenandunwin.com

National Library of Australia
Cataloguing-in-Publication entry:

Herald, Justin.
  Forget the elephants, watch out for the fleas.

  ISBN: 978 1 74175 691 3 (pbk.)

  Motivation: Success in business: Leadership

658.409

Set in 12/16 Sabon by Midland Typesetters, Australia
Printed in Australia by McPherson's Printing Group

10 9 8 7 6 5 4 3 2 1

The most successful men in the end are those whose success is the result of steady accretion. It is the man who carefully advances step by step, with his mind becoming wider and wider—and progressively better able to grasp any theme or situation—persevering in what he knows to be practical, and concentrating his thought upon it, who is bound to succeed in the greatest degree.

Alexander Graham Bell

CONTENTS

Introduction 11
1 That dreaded 1% 19
2 Small issues can equal big problems—
  the fleas 33
3 Don't make the elephants bigger than
  they actually are 45
4 The art of personal minesweeping 59
5 The snowball effect 71
6 Empty your recycle bin every now
  and then 85
7 How to move on and past those fleas 97

You never know how many apples there are in a seed.

INTRODUCTION

The purpose of this book is simple. Most people's problems start out as small as a flea, but too often those problems or issues are left alone and eventually become as huge as an elephant. This book has been written to help you understand and address the 'small' things in your life so you can reach your desired goals without too many disruptions.

If you were to go to Africa on safari, the guide wouldn't have to spend a lot of time pointing out the elephants. Why? Because they are so big that you can't miss them—you can see those elephants coming from a long way off. It is the same with the big issues in your life. You probably don't need someone to point out your own big issues as you already know what they are.

Forget the elephants, watch out for the fleas

Now a flea is a different story. Fleas are tiny, they cause a great deal of irritation and it takes a lot of searching and concentration to find one. This is the same with the 'fleas' of your life. Some little issues will need to be searched for and may take some time to find, but unless you address these little areas they can add up to one major headache. Ignorance solves nothing. Each and every one of you reading this book has to take control over the little issues before they blow out and cause major disruptions to your life. Sure, some of those 'fleas' may take a bit of work to track down, but be diligent and you will reap the benefits. Time and concentration is the key here. Spend some time reading this book and concentrate on ridding yourself of the small things that keep on popping up in your life and creating bigger problems.

Each of us has DNA that makes us who we are. DNA is a structure that carries the genetic information that makes up an individual. That is why we are all different to each other. When it comes to reaching success in our lives, I believe that we all have our own individual 'success DNA' as well. By that, I mean instead of trying to be like someone else, copying what others have done or learning how they did it, maybe we

Introduction

should concentrate on trying to understand our own success DNA. You need to understand that your way is your way when it comes to success. This in turn means that you, the individual, need to work on every aspect of who you are. This includes the good, the not so good, the big issues (the elephants), the small issues (the fleas) and, at some point in time, areas that haven't popped up yet.

I am constantly talking to people about how they can reach their particular goals. It always shocks me that many people seem to think that success is going to come to them by doing it someone else's way instead of making it work themselves. Now this, I have to say, is a natural way to think if you don't understand that you have your own success DNA within you. Your success DNA is what helps you reach your goals regardless of how other people have reached theirs. As you will see throughout this book, if there are issues that you have left unaddressed, these issues will eventually slow you down or stop you dead in your tracks. Your job is to find and highlight these little 'fleas', remove them from your life and move on to what you desire.

Remember the Frank Sinatra song 'My Way'? That is exactly how you need to approach success as well as any areas that you need to work on. Sure, there will be a whole lot that you won't know or understand along the way—that will be the case with anything you are trying for the first time—but don't let that stop you from starting.

When I started my first business, Attitude Inc., I had no idea what I was doing. To be honest I didn't really think it would go very far, but I wanted to give it a crack and I figured I would just do it my way and see where it led me. I must admit the result was a pretty good one.

Now, if you ask some people today, they will still say that the way I went about business was wrong. But for me, I just look at the end result. This is the same for you right now. The right way to reach success is the way that works and the wrong way is the way that doesn't. I realise that may sound overly simplistic, but it is the truth. That is why you need to trust and believe that you have your own success DNA. It is what makes your success yours and, ultimately, it is what makes you, you.

Once you start experiencing some success, I guarantee it will spur you on to try harder and harder. But copying other people will only lead you to frustration. Just because someone else makes a success of their life a certain way does

Introduction

not mean that you will experience the same success by copying them. We all have our own little fleas to address. If you copy someone else you will address areas you have in common with them but leave other areas particular to you exposed, which will eventually cause problems. You have to put your stamp of ownership on your own success. I bet you will be amazed at the results you can achieve by doing things your way.

So instead of trying to find out what the new methods, courses, approaches or theories are when it comes to reaching your own goals, why not back yourself and try it your own way. Who knows, you may already have all the skills and characteristics that you need apart from a bit of self-belief and the willingness to work on those small areas that may have been stopping you up until this point.

Success is not for the select few, it is for the ones who decide to go out there and get it their way and who constantly self-assess to ensure that they are always working on making themselves better. Throughout this book you will see that there are many small things that can throw our lives off track. By applying what you are about to read, you will be able to address some of those 'fleas' once and for all and move past the issues

Forget the elephants, watch out for the fleas

that may have been holding you back. You deserve to live the life you dream of, but at times it will require a lot of work. Those who experience their dreams are the ones who have pushed on and past their issues to reach their goals.

> 1

THATDREADED**1%**

Isn't it amazing that when we least expect something to happen, or more so when we can't afford for something to happen, it happens? Right at that moment when things seem to be going perfectly, it all falls apart. I am constantly amazed by what I call the one per cent principle. What is the one per cent principle you ask? Have you ever been in a situation when someone says to you that something is a ninety-nine per cent certainty to work, which in turn means that there is only a one per cent chance that it won't work out, and then that dreaded one per cent gets in the way and ruins that perfectly good ninety-nine per cent certainty? Let's be honest at the start of this book—it is the one per cent that we all need to be aware of because, realistically, that one per cent is what most of us never even bother looking out for. It is the little things that cause the major issues in our lives. Those little things, while they remain unseen, are the reason that many people keep battling with the same issues over and over again.

Many people just go through life with a 'she'll be right, mate' mentality, hoping they can get by with a majority ruling. By that I mean they hope and pray that if the majority of problems are sorted out and taken care of, then the leftover smaller issues will be outweighed by the success of the major challenges and everything will just work out for the best. For those people, it's a 'cross your fingers, shut your eyes and hope for the best' approach, which rarely gets anyone anywhere.

There is an old proverb that says 'it's the little foxes that spoil the vines and the vineyards'. To me that says it's the little things that can't be seen from a quick glance that need to be looked for and rooted out of our lives. Otherwise our life journey, hopes, dreams and aspirations will be undermined and ruined by those pesky little things that, if acknowledged and addressed, could be fixed and eradicated, leaving you free to focus your time and attention on the important things.

I also have to say that the majority of little things that get in our way are, most of the time, of our own creation. Sure, it is nice when we can blame others for why we didn't reach our goals, but the reality is that we ourselves need to take ownership of our aspirations. We need to start accepting that the one per cent can be worked on by us and that we are the ones who created these 'small' problems in the first place.

Let's have a look at some of the little things that can stop your journey dead in its tracks. (I have only listed a few here or we'd be going for hours.) Impatience, frustration, lack of self-belief, listening to anyone and everyone who gives you their opinion, our reactions and over-reactions to situations and comparing yourself to other people are just some examples of small foxes. To some people they will seem like surface or small issues that can be overcome and not relevant to the overall picture of what they want to achieve, but for others these small foxes have the ability to stop them from achieving anything because these people give up believing that they will. The reason I have said 'give up believing that they will', is because there is a tendency for some people to be over-aware that something small might ruin what they are trying to achieve. Or perhaps in the past when things haven't worked out the way they hoped, maybe even just once due to something small, sometimes that 'failure' seems to stick with them as a constant reminder that they might fail the next time they try something. This in turn makes them act in a way that will subsequently force them down a path that they don't want to go down all due to the fact that their revised thinking and actions dictate that unwanted outcome. Once you understand what it is you need to fix or rectify, you can get back on track and back to reaching the goals you want to reach.

One thing that I constantly see as a big hurdle for people who sit in front of me wanting my advice is the area of unrealistic expectations. Now before you start sending me letters criticising me about not encouraging people to think big, let me explain. While I am a very big believer in thinking big and aiming high, too many times people get so caught up in that process that they don't sit back and compare what they would *like* to achieve and what they *can* achieve. The issue with aiming too high from the start is that it could be the total undoing of your journey and ambitions if you have aimed too big. That small and simple factor can stop you cold. It comes

That dreaded 1%

back to the one per cent. Sure, ninety-nine per cent of your desires are that big, but when the rubber hits the road and you finally realise that you have to actually live up to those ambitions and work a whole lot harder in order to reach them, the dreaded one per cent starts to outweigh the other ninety-nine per cent.

It is like looking to buy a car. You go out and shop around at various dealers—you have your budget, you know what you can afford and you are adamant that you are going to stick to your budget—and somehow you get caught up in the excitement of seeing all of these beautiful motor vehicles that are one or two steps ahead of what you can afford and, with the added pressure of the sharp and skilful salesman, you are tempted into buying one of them. And because you are so caught up in the moment you seem happy with what you're just done. Now, over the following few weeks you really look after that car—after all, you are now living a dream. You clean it every day and one time you even catch yourself saying goodnight to it. You are in love with your new purchase as it is everything that you have ever wanted. Then the time comes to start making those payments. Now you are facing a problem due to you spending above the amount

Forget the elephants, watch out for the fleas

you knew you could afford. You are under a lot of pressure. You start realising that the purchase, although it made you feel good at the time, may have been a mistake. You start having second thoughts about the same purchase that only days before you were over the moon about. That car that you loved has now become a source of frustration and pain. You end up regretting and resenting everything about it due to the amount of extra work that is now required to keep it, which you never even considered at the time.

A lot of people experience a similar scenario in other areas of their lives. At the start, they are so gung-ho about aiming for the stars and accomplishing all that they set their minds to, but when the reality sets in of what they will need to do to not only keep that dream going but expand upon those desires, the shine wears off and they start resenting that they even started on that journey in the first place. They then allow resentment or frustration to creep in. That negativity (the little foxes) starts having a major effect on their desires and dreams (the vineyard). They start regretting everything about what they are doing and reflecting poorly on their outcomes in general instead of just focusing their attention on the areas that are causing them pain.

That dreaded 1%

Many people have goals. For some, their goals and aspirations are reachable and sensible. But for others, their goals are so out there and so far out of their reach that there really isn't much hope that they will be achieved in the desired time frame if at all.

As I said before, I am always coming across people whose goals are so huge and so removed from reality that all they have done is set themselves up for disappointment. They mistakenly believe that they need to get everything they desire straightaway or they will be failures. They want a champagne lifestyle while they are barely scraping by on a beer budget. If only they saw their desired goals as stepping stones and not destinations, maybe one day they would achieve them.

Now, I too would like the fancy schmancy things as well. I would love to own an Aston Martin DB9 (just to be like James Bond), and while I am at it I would like to take a few years off and travel the world first class with my family to wherever we chose to go. Oh, and one last thing: I would love to have membership in Qantas' Chairman's Lounge just because it is by invitation only and I don't think I will be invited any time soon. But do you know what? These things probably aren't going to happen in the very short-term future. These are things that I would love to have, but I don't let being without them shape or dictate my current happiness with my life. Does that mean that I give up, pack up everything, chuck a tantrum in the corner and begrudge everyone else who has achieved those things? NO! It just means that I need to concentrate on how I can work my way to one day maybe achieving those things. Please note the word 'maybe'.

I need to live in the land of 'now' instead of the land of 'if only'. What that does for me is make me concentrate on the present. By focusing all of my attention on things that, in reality, are so far from my grasp will only ensure that I become more disheartened on a daily basis. It also means that I will stop focusing on the things that I could do today that will make me happier right now.

Does this mean that I then give up on those luxuries that I desire? Not at all. It just means that I need to concentrate on getting the day-to-day tasks and goals achieved so that I can work my way towards those things that, at this stage, are out of my reach. By acknowledging the reality of your current situation, you can then address the areas that need addressing. Slowly and surely you can work towards your huge goals.

You know, I may never obtain those things that I mentioned before, but as I have numerous smaller goals, I am able to continue to have personal success every year, every month, every week and every day. If my only goals were those big things, you can easily see how my life would become frustrating, which is not what life is about.

Along those lines, if all I do is focus on the big picture and not address the little things that may stop my progress, I risk sabotaging my journey right from the start. Now that said, while it is great that you now realise that it is the small things that can actually slow you down or even stop you, unless you act upon addressing them, you will never get on top of things and will find them a constant thorn in your side.

Think about the following statement: Life rewards completions not intentions. Too many people 'intend' to get themselves to a better place either financially or personally, or to work on their relationships or lose weight, just to name a few examples. We can all go through life with the greatest of intentions, but unless we act upon them and complete what we intended to do, those intentions are just fanciful and hollow ideas.

I am yet to meet anyone who is living a life full of success who has not acted upon the desires

Forget the elephants, watch out for the fleas

they once had. Success doesn't just fall in your lap. It takes precise and deliberate actions. A lot of people intend on making their lives work out the way they had originally planned, but intending and acting are two totally different things.

Your intentions will set a direction for you to start from. Don't forget that in order for anyone to accomplish anything, there needs to be an intention from the start. That is really the point that I want to make here. Your intentions are the starting point of your journey towards your goals and dreams. Without intention there is no potential direction or movement. But don't stall once you've identified your intentions. Get up and get going, press on towards the goals you set for yourself. Intentions, desires and goals go hand in hand. Without a goal your desire to achieve is one-dimensional. That is why intention is important. It is the spark that brightens up the path that you need to follow.

Intentions are like turning on your car lights when driving in the dark. They show a way. Up until that point, you have a somewhat darkened outlook. When your intentions are clear to you they act like a directional path. Now it may turn out that you need to deviate from your perceived course along the way but don't sweat it—at least you are moving. This is where your goals kick in. You have set your course and know where you want to go, so no matter what happens to you along the way, ensure that you keep aiming towards your desired outcomes.

Your intentions are governed by the present. By that I mean, your desires for the future and their possible outcomes have to be dealt with and understood from where you are right now, today, as you read this book.

Once you have established your intentions, don't stop until you have completed what you have started. Sure there may be instances where you need to stop due to unforeseen circumstances (there's that blasted one per cent again), but make sure you get back on that horse and keep moving. I have met many people who have the world's greatest intentions, but that means nothing if there has been no action towards completing those intentions. Make sure you are not just a dreamer. Don't sit around living in the world of 'what if'. Move past that and operate and live in the world of 'I did it'.

Too many people live their lives through a series of events. If things are good then everything is good for them, but if things are bad then it is the end of the world. Life rewards those who

Forget the elephants, watch out for the fleas

push past the issues. Life isn't measured by our experiences, whether good or bad, or our intentions. It is measured by what we complete.

So what do you need to complete? If that one per cent keeps getting in your way and slowing you down, then it is time to start focusing on those small issues that are making a big impact. It's your job to find out what that one per cent that keeps stopping you is made up of.

\> 2

SMALL ISSUES CAN EQUAL BIG PROBLEMS —THE FLEAS

I am not sure about you, but my big issues can sometimes either take care of themselves or are easily worked out due to their size. It is the small issues, the ones that you either don't see coming or have overlooked for a long time, that you need to be aware of. The time you have spent in preparation for achieving your life goals will be shown when you attempt to live those dreams. If the small issues have not been worked through, your outcomes and desires, big and small, will be short-lived or not realised at all.

In this chapter I want to focus on the small issues that you might have in your life—the ones you may not have even seen yet or have ignored for a period of time thinking that they aren't an integral part of you. I call these small things *fleas*.

Fleas are tiny little creatures that, due to their size, can move around with ease and speed. They have a series of combs and bristles all over their body which allows them to hang on to what they are attached to. They belong to the order of insects called Siphonaptera which literally means 'wingless siphon'. They may be small but they can have a huge impact. After all, fleas were responsible for spreading the bubonic plague (Black Death) throughout the world. It amazes me that such a small thing had such a huge effect. The other thing that needs to be pointed out is that if a flea bites you, it can take a while for you to feel the effects of the bite.

That is why I refer to our small issues as fleas. Sure they may seem minor to us, so minor in fact that most times we overlook them. But as with a flea, unless you take care of them, these small issues will have a huge effect on you and your life. The small issues can stick to you and suck out your life and passion unless you deal with them once and for all. They have the potential to siphon your energy to a point that you give up due to the amount of stuff going wrong and the feeling that nothing seems to be working out for you.

Small issues can equal big problems—the fleas

As with a real flea's bite, you may not really feel the effects of the small issues that are there right now, but over time they will make their way to the surface. Odds are those small things will appear at the time that you can't afford anything to go wrong and will potentially cause a huge problem. If left alone, the small issues can become an enormous stumbling block and lead you to thinking that it is all too hard and giving up.

The tricky thing about your small issues or problems is that, because they are so tiny (often insignificant in your own eyes), you may tend to ignore them or even believe that they will just go away and work themselves out. That is a big mistake. Now, not that I was there, but I would hazard a guess that back when the bubonic plague started, if someone was to point out a little flea as the potential killer of over 25 million people, I am sure that they would have been laughed out of town.

It all comes down to perspective. To you, it may seem like a small issue that isn't worth worrying about, but if you put it into perspective, which will require a greater degree of focus on the situation than you might normally give it, it may be more important and potentially more damaging to your goals and dreams than you originally thought. That is why we all need to ensure our perspective is true and clear.

Let me explain. At the beginning of each year my family and I all go away on a holiday. Even though we might go away during the year on small getaways, the New Year's holiday is the one where we just shut off from everything around us. One year we decided to go to Fiji. We decided on Treasure Island so that I could wear my pirate outfit and eyepatch all day. Well, not really, but we liked the seclusion and what it had to offer, so off we went. It was a great holiday with the kids as all we did was hang out all day doing, well, nothing. We spent a lot of time snorkelling in the crystal-clear waters. One day, as we were snorkelling, I saw a reef shark. Now I have to say I am not up-to-date on my shark species and I really had no idea what was swimming underneath me, but just the sight of it freaked me right out. It wasn't until we got out of the water later that a local told me that it was 'fairly harmless' (whatever *fairly* means).

When I first saw the shark it looked like the size of a bus—I mean it was huge. Then, as I got water in my goggles and had to tread water while I emptied them, I put my head under the water without my goggles on and through the haze I

Small issues can equal big problems—the fleas

could see that the shark was a whole lot smaller than I had thought. You see, the goggles really magnified what I was looking at under that water. This is the same with some of the problems we face. We can all have 'goggles' on, which in turn magnifies or distorts what we are looking at. Looking at our dilemmas, dramas or issues through tainted and unrealistic eyes can throw a whole lot of confusion into a particular situation.

We all need to have the right perspective on our situations. Believing what you first see may cause you to believe your issues are bigger than they really are. The opposite is true as well. It may be like looking through a telescope from the wrong end and the thing you are focused on seems to have shrunk considerably in size. The problem with that is we can tend to ignore something that might seem small but in reality could be a potential problem.

A lot of the time our perspective is formed purely from our perceptions. We think a certain situation is what it is so we then form our perspective on that situation which in turn becomes fact to us. So what do we do if our perception is nowhere near the actual reality of a situation? This is just like my shark story. If I hadn't figured out that my goggles had altered my vision and that everything was not as big as it seemed, then odds are I would not have gone back in the water. I would have been afraid to come in contact with another 'huge' sea creature. The same goes with your own situations. You need to stop, stand back and re-address the situation you are in. Take a fresh and clearer look at what you are seeing. You may be surprised to see that things are not as bad as you first thought they were. You may also find that the small issue that is hanging around is actually a dream killer unless addressed and fixed.

This clearer perspective will then assist you in working on your desires without slowing or stopping your progress. You will be a lot more focused on an outcome, a conclusion and a result because you will now know what you are supposed to be working on in order to achieve it as well a sits overall importance to the bigger picture of your life.

These days we all seem to be running around like chickens with our heads cut off, never seeming to have enough time in the day to complete what we need to get done. It seems as though as soon as we start something that is really important and really urgent, something else pops its head up which we feel is equally as

Small issues can equal big problems—the fleas

important, which in turn leads us to try to do everything at the same time, ultimately resulting in having half-completed tasks all over the place.

This hectic feeling doesn't only effect our time management, but also our ability to make correct decisions on important matters. We can sometimes rush in with an answer or solution that really isn't the right one all because we want to solve the problem as quickly as we can. This sense of having no time can also force us to only focus on the glaringly obvious things in our lives instead of hunting for the small issues that may be adding to our feeling of being out of control.

So how can you make sure you are making wise choices? How can you find out what it is that is stopping you getting ahead and through your current situation? Well, the answer is really a simple one. So simple that most people overlook it as they think there needs to be a deeper or harder solution. What you need to do is address the level of importance of every decision you need to make, every choice that you have and every aspect of your journey through life. Many people make haphazard choices for their lives which lead them further away from resolving their issues and getting ahead. All they do is address the surface things—you know, the big issues that stand out like elephants—instead of looking deeper. When you understand how important things really are, you will naturally take more time and care in coming up with a solution that will add value to your situation.

I have a friend who has been going through a financially tough time lately. While he has been working very hard at getting himself back on track, he has had to learn the principle of the *level of importance* the hard way. He was going from bad decision to bad decision all because he thought that any answer he could come up with on the spot was a good one. He never addressed the level of importance of the different decisions he had to make on a daily basis to decide which problem had to be solved first and which problems or decisions weren't that relevant to his current predicament. He was also trying to do everything at once, which meant that he never focused on one thing at a time as he was trying to keep everything from falling apart around him. He was only doing surface stuff instead of looking for the underlying causes. He was so busy dealing with the big issues that he never made any time to hunt for the fleas (the small but potentially potent issues).

It wasn't until I sat down with him after he had had enough that we laid it all out on the table and

Small issues can equal big problems—the fleas

started to get some perspective. He went through the areas and decisions that he had to make each day to overcome his financial situation, and what we found was that he was spending most of his time on the surface issues that weren't actually impacting in a positive way on his financial problem. Basically, he felt that it was better to look as though he was doing something, even if what he was doing wasn't helping him.

Once we put the surface issues to one side and identified the main problems, we were able to address those issues by ranking them from most important to least important. Now he had clarity.

If you are going through a tough time where you can't seem to see the forest for the trees, just stop for a minute, write a list of the areas that need addressing and then work out which of those areas are the most important/urgent and which ones aren't. This will then give you a direction to head in instead of feeling like you are going around in circles all the time.

Sure, you may have been moving, but realistically you haven't gone anywhere. It is time to take control and understand that there is a level of importance to everything that we do. All you need to do is figure out what needs to go at the top of the list.

Forget the elephants, watch out for the fleas

Just as fleas are known as wingless siphons, you may find that those small issues you haven't stopped to identify may be sucking the life out of your dreams and goals and zapping away all of your energy every day. You may realise that things aren't working out the way that you had planned, and yes, you may be trying very hard to find those individual things that you think are getting in the way, but what you need to do is look very closely at every aspect of your life. Not only the way you go about things, but also your attitudes, actions and your mindset. You need to hunt for those fleas. You need to stop casting a casual eye over your life to find the obvious things and start carefully and thoroughly going through every part of your life. It is the same as if you were trying to see if your dog had fleas. You wouldn't stand back and make an assumption from a distance; you would need to check carefully through his fur, being ever so attentive, to see if there were any there.

You really need to be ruthless and not skim over things. You will need to look in places that you may have assumed were all okay—for example, your attitudes, your work ethic or your relationships with other people. You also need to look at the way you react to situations when put

Small issues can equal big problems—the fleas

under pressure and the way you view your own abilities to get to where you want to go in life.

As stated throughout this chapter, if you decide to brush over the small issues, one day they may be the thing that stops your journey. That would be a real shame if it was something that was once so small that it could have been fixed quickly and effectively.

> 3

DON'T MAKE THE ELEPHANTS BIGGER THAN THEY ACTUALLY ARE

It is natural to focus on the big issues in your life. Situations such as losing your job, having financial issues, relationship break-ups or maybe even having a lack of direction can take up a lot of your time. But the purpose of this chapter is to try to get you to see how some of these things can take care of themselves. In fact they may have needed to happen in order for you to move on to the next part of your life.

I call these big issues and problems 'elephants'. There is no mistaking an elephant—you can see it from a long distance away. It is most unlikely you would go up to the elephant enclosure at the zoo and think to yourself, 'Hmmm, now where are those elephants?' You can't miss them—they are huge. This is the same for those big issues you will come across in your life. They will be so big that you won't be able to miss them, no matter how hard you try. That being the case, you need to deal with those issues quickly and with precision in order to get your life's journey back on track.

The problem that most people create for themselves is that, because some of these problems are huge, they tend to focus all of their time and energy on them which then leaves little to no time to focus on the smaller issues (as was discussed in the previous chapter). Let's take a minute to look back and reflect on a major issue in your life that popped up say last year and took you by surprise and made you think that you would not be able to move on from it. When I use this example with people I am mentoring I ask them one question: What did you do about that major issue when it presented itself? Most of the time the answer I am given is: 'I panicked, as I had no idea what to do due to it being a big problem or issue that was not planned for.'

Please don't think for a minute that I am saying that you should ignore the major issues in your life, but my point is that sometimes those 'major issues' aren't as big as you think and most of the time they have a natural course to run. The one guarantee I can give you is that at some point in time you will face major challenges in your life. The key to keeping your momentum is to see them for what they are and not to make them bigger by focusing all of your attention on them.

There is one thing that I love doing, and that is driving. Whether it is going to get milk or bread from the service station or driving a long way to a conference I am speaking at, I just love it. I love the freedom that driving gives me. Recently I had been away overseas for a holiday and I couldn't wait to get back and go for a drive. On the day we landed I came home from the airport, did the 'good husband' thing where you help to unpack all the suitcases and then I decided to go for a drive. All seemed to be going well—the sun was shining, there were only a few cars on the road—and then suddenly, 'BANG'! I hit a pothole.

Now I never saw it coming but it was a beauty. I mean it was huge; I was lucky that I didn't vanish down it. I pulled over to see if I still had the front wheel on my car and everything seemed to look okay. As I started driving again I noticed

Forget the elephants, watch out for the fleas

that my steering wheel was now way off centre and the car was pulling to the left badly. The next day I took it into my local tyre shop and they fixed it up with a wheel alignment.

So what's the point of this story you ask? Well, it is a simple principle. You see, many people travel through life going about things the way they always have, cruising along, and then suddenly, 'BANG!' out of nowhere things start going wrong. Whether it is finances, relationships or your emotions, things stop going straight and if you take your hands off your personal wheel you know that your outcomes will be way off course, just as my car decided to consistently pull to the left after hitting 'Gigantor' the pothole.

This is why we all have to be aware, first, that there are personal potholes out there that we can all hit every now and then, and secondly, if you do run into a bit of a drama in your life, you need to ensure you straighten things out as soon as you can. Otherwise, as with the tyres on my car, if the problem is left untreated, you may end up causing yourself and your goals a whole lot more damage.

As I was watching the guys realign my wheels I noticed that while the initial impact was harsh and sudden, the realigning of my wheels was precise and calculated. This is how you have to be if you are trying to get yourself back on track after hitting one of life's potholes. Don't be tempted to rush in and do the first thing that pops into your head to get yourself back on track. Just like the technicians who fixed my car, you need to be deliberate about finding the solution to realigning your direction. It may only take a little tweaking to affect a great and positive change on your situation.

Now, most problems can be solved and most dramas can be fixed, but you first need to acknowledge that your direction may be a little off centre due to those potholes (dramas, issues or problems) you may have encountered along the way. Just make sure you have people around you who understand the mechanics of getting your personal alignment back to centre. These people could be close friends or professionals you look up to.

Sure, this large pothole unsettled my car in a major way, and yes, I had to address it sooner rather than later, otherwise I would have created even more damage, but it would be exactly the same if I left a whole lot of smaller issues with my car to another day. After a period of time those smaller issues would build up to create a major headache for me.

Forget the elephants, watch out for the fleas

The problem that most people end up creating for themselves is that they only address the major 'potholes' of their lives—when things seem to go BANG!—which is understandable, but you need to remember that while some of the smaller issues in your life (the fleas) may not have the same initial impact, if left unaddressed they can add up to create a huge drama for you. And you may be surprised to read this, but the solutions to some of your issues may be in front of you right now.

I have recently come to the conclusion that I must be getting older! Yes, I realise that that will happen automatically, but the other day I had one of those experiences that my parents used to have when I was younger. I was working in my office, chugging through all of the paperwork that had been piling up, and then I had to find my stapler to put things in their proper order. I searched high and low for that wretched lump of metal. I even looked in places where I knew it wouldn't be just in case it was there. No matter where I looked I just couldn't find it. I then sat on my chair with a sense of utter despair—my ergonomically designed office equipment had beaten me. I had to accept defeat. Then I glanced to the side of my computer and there it was! The stupid thing was right in front of my face the whole time. I mean, how could I have missed it?

Sometimes when we face issues, problems or dramas in our lives, especially when we are trying to reach certain levels of success for ourselves, we tend to run around madly trying to find a solution to our issue. What we all need to do is take a chill pill and slow down and be strategic for a minute.

You see, when we are in a fluster about something, when things haven't gone according to the way we thought they would or when we start thinking too much about an issue, we can tend to start running around in circles. We focus on trying to come up with a solution for our predicament when in fact what we need to do is slow down, clear our thoughts and approach it with a rational mind in order to get a rational solution. You may find when you do this that the answer you were looking for was right in front of your face the whole time.

If only I had approached finding my stapler in a structured and concise manner, instead of rushing around in a flap, I would not have wasted all of that energy and got myself so frustrated. While I realise that this example may seem trivial, you would be surprised to see how many people get very frustrated over things that may seem

Forget the elephants, watch out for the fleas

huge to them at the time but in reality aren't that big a deal. So the next time things seem to build up to a crisis point and you realise you are wasting a lot of time trying to solve a problem that perhaps wasn't that big in the first place (a flea that you have transformed into your own elephant), and you can see that you are just running around in circles with no actual positive outcome, just stop for a minute. Think about doing something else for a little while and re-approach it with a clearer head. You may find the answer right in front of you.

Understand that if you focus too hard on the big things they end up seeming a lot bigger, which is why you may feel overawed all the time. The reality might be that the elephants aren't as big as you think. You may be standing so close to the problem that it is all you can see. Move back a little and it might give you a better perspective and understanding of how to overcome the issues you are facing. As stated in the previous chapter, I believe our focus needs to be on the little things (the fleas) more so than the big things. The last thing that you want to do is make rash decisions over matters that could be easily corrected or fixed in a simple and timely manner.

Sometimes when things aren't going according

to plan we can tend to overreact. The problem with that is we can end up down the very path we were trying to avoid in the first place.

I have met and helped many people who have applied a *permanent solution to a temporary problem,* which in turn led them to regret their decisions once the dust settled a bit. By overreacting to a temporary problem, they then had to live with the permanent outcomes of the 'solution' to their problem. Once they actually saw this, you could see the look of disappointment on their faces as they realised their initial problem was nowhere near as extreme as their perceived solution. It was their haste to get out of one predicament that ended up leading them to another one down the track.

While it is fine and dandy for me to state this, I realise that sometimes some people think and feel that they have no other option in some situations other than a drastic one. That is why, before you make any major changes in your life, you need to make sure you have explored many options before you make a decision. Life is just like a game of chess. It has to be well thought out before you make a move!

Always remember that, in this case, time is your best friend and not your enemy. Rushing in and making a hasty decision will not mean that a problem or situation will go away. Sometimes, as the cowboys in the old westerns used to say to their horses, 'Whoa there, Nelly' is the reaction we need to have. Just slow it all down. The last thing that you would want is to close a chapter of your life before it has finished being written. Without sounding too flippant, and as stated before, most of the 'major' problems that we all face aren't as big as we think they are. I realise that there are some major personal issues that people will face, but I am not talking about those here. I am talking about the little issues that we tend to turn into major dramas all by ourselves.

When you are caught up in the middle of a crisis it may seem as though things are very bad, but if you take a step back for a minute, you may see things for what they truly are. Overreacting will only slow you down in the long run.

Recently, I met up with a woman and her husband who were after some of my advice. They were experiencing the outcomes of a permanent solution to a temporary problem and they had just figured that out. It turned out that around three months before our meeting the wife had lost her job. They had a huge mortgage and decided that they should sell up and move interstate—just like that! There was no serious thought process behind this decision at all. I thought this was a drastic move so I asked why they thought that they needed to make such a major change, to which they replied that they 'just panicked'. I asked whether she had tried to get another job and she answered 'No'. Now, I am not sure about you, but personally I would have thought that would have been the first thing to do rather than sell up and move out.

You see, instead of taking a moment to properly assess their situation, their actions—or, better put, reactions—had put them in a position they were miserable in. All they saw was the elephant and by overreacting they ended up with a lot of fleas to deal with. They could have easily begun to overcome that 'huge' problem in a very short time had they put it all into perspective.

Their situation may be a bit different to where you are at right now, but make sure you look at all of your options when things go a bit south for you. There would be nothing more frustrating than to find out that an overreaction caused you had even more restrictions or problems than if you had just worked through the original issues in the first place.

Forget the elephants, watch out for the fleas

Have you ever created a permanent solution to a temporary problem? If so, learn from those choices and understand that sometimes the big things may take care of themselves due to them having a natural course to run. By focusing on the huge issues all the time, maybe you are also causing them to hang around. It is now time for you to work these big issues out and get moving with the rest of your life.

>4

THE ART OF PERSONAL MINESWEEPING

I was watching a documentary on television a few years back on the minesweepers used by navies during wars at sea. What the minesweepers did (in layman's terms) was drag special cutting wire behind them which, when it came into contact with a sea mine that was moored to the ocean floor, would cut the mooring, which in turn would cause the mine to float to the ocean's surface where it could then be blown up by the crew aboard one of the minesweeping vessels. The sea mines sat under the surface of the ocean out of sight. So without the minesweepers an unsuspecting ship could be in danger of exploding one at any point in time. They say that the cost of producing those mines was anywhere from a half to ten per cent of the cost of removing them and that it took up to two hundred times as long to clear the minefield as to lay it. So, simply speaking, the mines were small objects that caused a huge impact.

Now you may be wondering why I have mentioned this. Well, sometimes it seems we all lay down mines in our lives. Things such as our attitudes, actions, reactions or other personal issues can have a huge impact on our future success. While it may have taken little time for them to become a part of your life, the fact is they may take many times longer to remove and the cost to do this will be greater as well. The longer you wait to address these issues, the more effort will be required to remove them. You will use a whole heap of your time and energy that could have been better served working towards reaching your desires.

That is why we all need to employ the minesweeper theory in our lives. We need to constantly run over every aspect of our lives, cutting away some of those issues that lay just beneath the surface in order to get them to float to the top so that they can be removed once and for all. If we don't, chances are one day we will run into one of these 'personal mines' and they will create a whole lot of unnecessary damage

The art of personal minesweeping

and drama. It is the potentially destructive things in our lives that hide under the surface that most people don't address. They live by the 'out of sight out of mind' theory, which in reality is a myth. As you can see with the sea mine example, problems that are 'out of sight' can still create huge damage once discovered.

Some people (maybe even you) don't realise that some of their issues are moored down below the surface and are somewhat fixed in their lives. That is why we all need to completely remove them by cutting all our ties to them. Knowing where our weaknesses and shortfalls are and actually taking steps to improve them are two totally different things. You need to take action and go on a mine-sweep through your life. Once you detect something that has the potential to do damage or cause you to slow down, you need to bring it to the surface and get rid of it once and for all.

It also has to be pointed out that sometimes you may run into 'sea mines' of someone else's doing. Some people around you may create problems in your life with or without any prior warning. Not all the relationships you will have in your life will be good ones. That is why you have to apply the same principle in those situations and run a *sweep* over these people to see if there is anything about them that may create dramas further down the track. You may need to cut your ties to those people so that you don't experience permanent damage from them at a later date.

Let me give you a personal example to explain exactly what I mean. Over the last few years I had a friend who, every now and then, would require a bit more attention than my other friends. This wasn't because they were in need of that attention but because they were demanding it. While I had a gut feeling right from the start that it could be a nightmare friendship, I never acted upon those feelings. Like most people, I obliged when I could and put up with it. Truth be told I was hoping that one day this person would see how very draining they were to others and address this for and by themselves. But they didn't. They actually turned things up a notch and started to become very demanding on not only my time but on other people's as well. I tried to assist where I could—I even placed myself in their business to lend a hand—but, ultimately, it all blew up in my face.

I started to hear feedback from others on comments this 'friend' was making about me.

The art of personal minesweeping

Now, from where I stood, all I ever did was the right thing by this person and to the greatest of my ability, so I was a bit miffed with what I was being told. As it is my nature to approach things head-on I confronted this person, but they said that the things I had heard weren't true so I just left it at that. But over many months following this confrontation the same issues kept coming up over and over again, so I cut the ties of that relationship and moved on with my own life. Had I kept that relationship in my life I would have continued to experience the same issues time and again, and it would have required more of my time and effort which, in turn, would have distracted me from my own life and desires.

Now, to be honest, I thought that once I cut those ties that would be the end of it, but unfortunately this person then started badmouthing me to anyone who would listen. Luckily, because I had severed all ties with this person, I was not affected in any way due to the distance I had created in our relationship.

One of my theories in life is that it is none of my business what people think of me. Accordingly, I have no problem with how this person carries on because I am bigger than the situation they are causing. I am not going to allow myself to sink to their level of operating as I am better off charting my own course.

So, while you will have to look for your own personal mines sitting under the surface in your life, make sure you look out for other people who may pop up and cause you grief and drama. Also, look out for those small things that don't cause huge amounts of damage straightaway but are just as annoying and potentially damaging in the long run. Which leads me to another car analogy . . .

Recently, after getting my car fixed from that pothole, I was driving along and every second or so I could hear a weird and annoying noise coming from the front. I pulled over and checked everywhere but couldn't see anything out of place, so I got back in and continued on my way. After a little while, I noticed the same noise and pulled over again. I looked at my front tyre and saw that I had run over a big nail on the road, which was now sticking out of my tyre and causing the strange sound. I subsequently took my car back to the tyre shop, got it fixed, and went on my way. If I didn't get it fixed, I would have had to have put up with that same sound every day and the damage from the nail may have ended up causing a major problem. Either way it was annoying and I had to address it.

The art of personal minesweeping

So what is the point of that you might ask? Well, every now and then when travelling along the road towards your personal goals, you may pick up a foreign object that could cause you to slow down or stop if not addressed in time. Just because it isn't as big as a sea mine doesn't mean it can't still slow you down unnecessarily.

The biggest problem is that, figuratively speaking, too many people leave the nails in their tyre, thinking such a small thing isn't going to affect them that much. But the issue with that is the longer you leave things untouched, the more annoying those issues will become and the more damage they can cause. Which is why we all need to be on the lookout for the 'nails' we may have picked up in our own lives.

There are many things we will come across throughout our lives that will be annoying and a source of frustration and which will slow us all down. Unless fixed, these issues and problems will create more dramas and turn into bigger problems. Attitudes, wrong feelings, frustrations and even relationships can all pick up 'nails'. I know someone who constantly picks up 'nails' in her life, and instead of removing them she leaves them there only to have them affect her outcomes every day.

Like with a car, every now and then we all need to do a once-around to ensure everything in our life is in working order. If you find something that shouldn't be there, get it out! If you think that checking yourself out every now and then is a waste of time, just imagine what it would be like having to sit and wait for the time it takes for things to get back on track.

One thing I am is impatient. When I took my car back to the tyre shop I had to wait while it was repaired. For me, that is pure frustration. I can't stand sitting around doing nothing when I know there are other things I could be doing. The same may happen to you if you ever pick up an emotional, attitudinal or relationship nail. Unless addressed straightaway, you may find yourself on the sidelines for some time while the damage is being repaired, and your progress up until that point will all but whittle away.

Now I didn't place that nail on the road, so I had no idea it was there. The same may happen to you in your personal life. Sometimes you may just pick up one of these things that can cause annoyance or frustration and there is nothing you can do about it. Don't get caught up in it for too long. Remove that annoying attitude, relationship or whatever it is and move on with your life.

The art of personal minesweeping

The secret here is to make sure you are fully aware of what is going on in your life and your journey every single day. Many people take their eyes off their personal goals, thinking that they will just get there one day or, even worse, they start to zone out from trying to reach the same goals for too long. A lot of the time, people have their lives on autopilot. Sure, they are heading in the right direction, but they are not taking a great deal of notice as to what is going on around them.

Have you ever been driving somewhere, and when you get to your destination you just can't remember how you got there, what roads you took, or even how many cars or people you passed on the way? While it was you who was driving the car, you were on autopilot and you made your way to your destination without paying much attention. Or even worse, you ended up somewhere you never wanted to go to at all, simply because you lost concentration and were on autopilot. That can be very dangerous while driving and the same goes for your personal journey as well.

Like in a car, if you don't seriously concentrate while you are working towards your goals, you may end up somewhere you never planned to be.

You could end up worse off than when you started, or you could run into a personal sea mine that stops you in your tracks so that you need to start all over again, losing all of that time and effort you had put in.

While many people get into a groove when working towards what they want to achieve in life, being fully focused on every part of the process and journey will pay off in the end. Concentrating while driving is a must; without it, other people's lives are at stake. In our own lives, if we lose concentration for just a while, the chances of someone else being at risk are minimal, but that loss in concentration can still take us far away from our intended goals.

Even if you do arrive at your proposed destination, by not having concentrated, the chances of you repeating that success a second or third time is fairly slim due to you not really knowing how you got there in the first place. I am not sure about you, but for me, I would prefer to learn from every experience instead of wasting time having to go over things again purely because I was off with the fairies.

When you drive a long distance it is advisable to stop every few hours to give yourself a break and regain your concentration. Why not apply

The art of personal minesweeping

that same principle to your personal journey? You may have been working towards a goal for so long that you can't remember when or why you actually started it. So why not have little rest breaks every now and then to refresh yourself and recharge your batteries? The last thing you want to do is to give up after putting in so much time and effort. Taking a break that allows you to switch your attention away from your goals may be just the thing you need. It doesn't mean that you aren't committed, it just assists you if working towards your goal is starting to become a labour instead of a desire.

Some goals may be easy to achieve and others are long-term. That is why you need to understand that when your goals start taking a long time to reach, make sure you stay focused, concentrate on the end prize and stay away from the autopilot switch. The last thing you want is to have your efforts up to this point go down the drain due to a momentary lack of attention.

So, whether it is a 'sea mine' or a 'nail on the road', make sure you are prepared to react as fast as you can to ensure you don't lose momentum. Have your personal minesweeper on 24/7 to ensure you find these issues before they find you.

> 5

THE SNOWBALL EFFECT

I am sure you understand what the snowball effect is. It is a term used to describe when something starts off small but gathers momentum and builds up and up to become a much bigger thing. Well, for the purpose of this chapter I am not referring to that type of snowball effect. What I am referring to has similar outcomes but, if properly managed, can aid you instead of hinder you.

As the snowball travels downhill it will pick up more speed, and it is this speed which causes some people's problems to keep getting bigger and bigger. So that is why I just had to address this principle in this book.

Let's call all of your dreams, aspirations, goals and future endeavours the snowball. So what we

Forget the elephants, watch out for the fleas

have right from the start may be a lot of things all combined, but at this stage the snowball will be quite small as it is based only on the resources you have right now.

So you have the snowball. It starts rolling and, as mentioned, it will start to get bigger and move faster depending on how hard you push it. This is where I have a different theory for you. Instead of worrying about the snowball for a minute, why not start addressing the gradient that the snowball is sitting on instead. Now, the steeper and clearer the gradient, the faster the snowball will travel by itself. My theory is not about you pushing and shoving the snowball along, but rather about working on your personal gradient and creating a path for your dreams to follow, less the junk that will slow them down.

Now you may be wondering what I mean by your personal gradient. This consists of everything that you are, including your attitudes, actions, thought processes, reaction times and relationships. If we all start working on the areas that can impact on our dreams and aspirations right from the start, maybe, just maybe, we will have a smoother run when we start working on achieving the things we want to achieve. Too many people think that their problems will work

The snowball effect

themselves out along the way. Well, this is definitely not the case. If left untreated, these areas will act like a huge log lying directly in your snowball's path, which has the potential to destroy all of the hard work you have put in.

As you may be starting to see, to some, these issues are just small annoyances, but let me give you a guarantee: they can slow the fastest moving person in a heartbeat. That is why you need to keep aware of the time you spend working on your problems. Maybe even outsourcing those little areas that have been an annoyance for a while may help to shortcut the process in the long run. Either way, these areas need to be found and worked on so you can then move on to the next issue. Spending too much time on something or constantly revisiting these problem areas will only slow you down.

The other day I arranged to get our house sprayed for spiders. I hate the little creatures—they freak me out big time. The following day I walked out to my driveway to retrieve my newspaper, as I do every morning, and I walked straight into a spider's web. So here I was doing the spider's web dance—you know, the one where you flap your arms around hysterically, brushing every part of your body, trying to remove all traces of that web as fast as you can. I came inside to the sound of loud laughter to find out that my entire family (if not the entire street) had been watching me go off in the front yard. I explained to everyone that I hate spiders as well as spider's webs, to which my eldest daughter Jade said, 'Just build a bridge, Dad, and get over it.' Build a bridge! Here I was fighting for my life on my front lawn from a potential killer spider and she was telling me to get over it?

Well, in reality there wasn't even a spider in the web, and even if there was, the web was a tiny one which probably would have meant that the spider would have been small as well. So what is the point of that story? Many of us go through life just doing what we do and doing it well. Then at some point we may run into something that either affects us in a negative way, throws us off balance or just upsets us. This is where 'choice' comes in to the equation. We all have a choice as to how we react and handle situations. You can either run around going off (figuratively speaking), flapping your arms about, telling anyone who is unfortunate enough to be within earshot about how hard done by you have been, why it isn't fair that the situation has happened to you or why you are the unluckiest person on the planet due to the amount of misery your life has produced—or you can build a bridge and get over your issues. To be honest, most of the 'issues' we have really aren't that big or damaging. We tend to blow them way out of proportion by focusing on them so much and building them up to be bigger than they really are.

What we all need to do when overcoming our issues or problems is follow my daughter's advice. We need to build a bridge and get over them. And then we need to go back and destroy that bridge so we don't constantly go backwards and forwards from our future to our past issues.

I have met a lot of people who don't want to let go of their past issues. They feel as though everything they have done in life (good and bad) makes them who they are today. That is so sad, as life is all about becoming better and overcoming our faults. They end up living a life filled with regret as they never seem to move on from past disappointments. I have said no to things in my past that sometimes I look back on and wish that I hadn't, but in reality I cannot change anything that has already happened.

I do not believe in regrets. Focusing on regrets forces us to live in the past. As I just said, I have been offered many opportunities that

I have chosen to pass on. Some of those opportunities have gone on to be major successes; some have gone on to fall in a big heap. If I was to live my life regretting all the things that could have been, I would just be torturing myself and making everyone around me miserable. You will never see the opportunities in front of you if you are looking back and reflecting on what is behind you. Your future is not in your past, so if you are still looking in that direction . . . TURN AROUND!

So, this week, find an old issue or a negative attitude that has been hanging around for a while and build a bridge and get over it. If it is an issue that has been plaguing you for some time, go back and destroy that bridge so you won't revisit it again. Life is too short to constantly battle with the same problems. I realise that some of this advice may be hard for some people to take in and act upon straightaway, but without action there are no results. That is why you need to have a plan of attack, so to speak. Don't approach this in a haphazard manner. Be deliberate and strategic.

As I have owned and run businesses for over fourteen years, I have had to operate most of my year according to my attack plan. Each year I need to plan ahead for the coming twelve months, as well as evaluate the year when it comes close to ending. I also apply the same principle to my personal life as well. I encourage you, when you get a bit of spare time, to perform the following 'business' check on your life.

1. Life plan

    With most businesses it is advisable to have a plan of attack so you know which direction you are headed in. This is the same for your personal life. Do you have a plan for where your life is heading? If you don't, maybe that is the reason you are constantly falling short of what you would like to achieve. Planning sets a structure in place; it gives you a perceived understanding of what may be needed to get you to where you would like to go. I have to say 'perceived' as not everything will work out the way you think it should, but it is better than being at the mercy of whatever ends up happening to you on a daily basis.

    Don't plan too much in advance, though. Sure, it is fine to have some big plans, but many people position their goals so far away that it takes forever to achieve them. If you don't get any results early in the process, you may choose to give up on those far away goals. That is why it is advisable to set small, medium and then larger goals into your plan. Achieving what you set out to achieve will give you a big lift, so make sure there are some immediate things in your plan to aim for. And don't forget to plan for when things don't work. By that I mean, plan now how you will react to disappointment or missed milestones. That way you won't waste too much time handling the shock or disappointment.

Lastly on this point, don't only have a 'Plan A'. Have a Plan B, C, D and so on. That way if the first thing doesn't work out the way you had planned, you will be able to move straight on to the next thing. This will help you ensure you don't lose momentum when things don't work out as planned.

2. Profit and loss

With a business it is advisable to regularly look at your profit and loss figures. You should do the same with your personal life and your personal journey. What have you personally gained this year and what have you lost? If you have gained the things you were trying to lose and lost the things you were trying to gain, then you are probably going in the wrong direction.

When you have a serious look at your life from this perspective, you will be able to make the necessary changes. Unfortunately, in a business context, many small business operators only check their profit and loss statement at the end of the year. By that time, if they are in trouble, it may be too late to do anything about it. So make sure you keep an eye on this area in your personal life. You need to be aware of and understand which areas you want and need to gain on in the year, as well as which areas you need to start clearing out.

3. Stocktake

With business, it is advisable to know exactly how much stock you have so that you don't run short. This assists with the continuous growth of that business because it avoids down time and loss of income. The same goes with your personal life. Why not stop for a minute and take stock of where your life is right now. Are you happy? Are there areas you could spend some time fixing? Are you where you want to be in life? There would be a million other questions I could throw in here but I am sure you get the point.

A lot of people may be too scared to have a stocktake on their life, in case they find out the actual truth. Don't be scared, just do it. Then you will know exactly where you stand. If you find things aren't where they should be, you will at least know and you will be able to address these areas and get back on track.

So as you can see, getting to where you want to go in life is not that hard, but it does require planning and it definitely requires discipline. And as you are the only person who is the CEO of your life, it is up to you to make it work the way you want it to.

In the last part of this chapter I want to touch on some little fleas that make a huge impact in people's lives. Those fleas are *assumptions*.

A lot of people make assumptions about their situations which lead them to either make unnecessary decisions or no decisions at all, all because they mistakenly believe their conclusions are fact. Assumptions lead to conclusions! Most assumptions are born out of feelings or reactions, which make you believe that the conclusion you came to

The snowball effect

is fact. This in turn makes you act or react in a certain way so that the assumption actually becomes a reality or fact. Now this is where things start getting messy. Due to the actions you took based on that first assumption, you have actually created a new reality without ever bothering to check if your assumption was correct in the first place.

I have met many people over the past few years through my mentoring program who have made major life-changing decisions purely based on assumptions, which led to them being in a position that was less than ideal. You may find if you look back on some aspects of your life you wish had never happened that they were created by you overreacting in certain situations and jumping to conclusions too quickly. Life isn't as black and white as we may like to think. There are no full stops in life, just commas. That is why, just like a comma, sometimes we all need to stop AND PAUSE to ensure we don't overreact in situations.

I bet if you took a serious look at those hard times in your life, you could now come up with various other ways you could have approached them. Look and see if you have created patterns in your life by overreacting or through hasty decision-making and you might start seeing where you could break those patterns once and for all.

Most people know what it is they would like to achieve. The key to achieving those desires is making sure you try to remove all of those obstacles that will stop that snowball from getting bigger and bigger so that your dreams became a reality.

>6

EMPTY YOUR RECYCLE BIN EVERY NOW AND THEN

One of the main reasons people struggle to move on and up towards what they desire is due to them holding on to some of the issues they may have faced in their past. While they may have overcome some of these issues, they nevertheless think they need to hang on to them for long periods of time. This one act can result in slowing down your progress because of the extra weight you're constantly lugging around.

Just like with a computer, every now and then we need to empty the recycle bins of our lives. Many people will go through various aspects of their lives and clean them out, but what they then do is they put those issues or areas of their lives into their own 'recycle bin' and fail to delete them altogether, even when those things are no longer of use to them.

A computer recycle bin is where you *temporarily* store the files you don't need anymore. However, if you don't empty that recycle bin from time to time all of that stuff you don't want or need starts taking up too much of the hard disc space and your system slows down. What you could do with that space if it was available would be a heck of a lot more than you could do with a system with limited and restricted ability.

This is the same for your personal life. There would be many of you reading this book right now who would have gone through issues in your life but not totally cleaned out some of the residual attitudes, feelings and resentments once and for all. The quicker you clean out these areas from your life, the more room you will have available for those things that will assist you to reach your desires rather than hinder you.

Some people may have an issue with this process because they seem to want to hang on to past hurts or feelings—like a trophy to remind them of how hard done by they think they were. Some people also use some of these past issues as a crutch to always excuse their current situations

Empty your recycle bin every now and then

and explain to everyone and anyone who will listen why they may still be struggling a bit.

The past is the past and that is where it needs to stay. In order for you to move on and in to what you desire, you will have to cut ties with some of your past issues. Having a mental recycle bin that you can still go back to and pick out some of that stuff and put it back into play in your life will do you no favours at all. All that will do is slow you down.

Recently I was talking to someone in an airport lounge as I waited for my plane to board. After talking about a lot of nothing, the conversation eventually became a bit deeper. This man went into detail about all of the dramas he had experienced in his past with his relationships, finances and even family matters. Now I have to say I really wasn't expecting the conversation to go down that path but it really seemed like he wanted to get some things off his chest. After about forty minutes of him downloading his past issues, failures and problems (his words) I asked him one question: 'What are you going to do with your future?' This question seemed to stump him. He took ages to answer me and then proceeded to tell me that his future was doomed no matter what he did because his past results had proven to him that life would never be kind to him. With that my plane was boarding and we departed.

On the plane home that day all I could think of was that conversation. I was particularly saddened by this man's outlook on his future. He could not see that he had a future worth looking forward to because he was taking his past results and projecting them onto his future results.

Your past has passed, as I stated before, so there is no need for you to constantly dig it up and relive what happened. Sure, some of the things that happened to us in our past will have a definite impact on us, but reliving them all the time will only cause you to slow down or even stop on your life's journey. It is a new day so why live an old life?

Too many people try to hang on to their past, intentionally or by default, all because it gives them an excuse as to why things haven't worked out up until that point. If you have past issues that are still holding you back then it is about time you put them to rest. It is as easy as deciding that you are not going back there.

Imagine you are going on an overseas trip. You arrive at the check-in counter at the airport and put your baggage on the weighing machine. As with all airlines, they have a set weight that they

Empty your recycle bin every now and then

allocate to each passenger for their bags. If your bags are overweight then there are two things that can happen. First, they will ask you to take some of your belongings out of your bags to make them compliant with the weight regulations. If that doesn't work or if you are not prepared to lighten the load, you will be hit with an excess-baggage charge. Your personal life works in a similar way.

We all need to get rid of some of the excess baggage in our lives. If we don't there will be a cost involved. That cost could be added attitudes (negative ones) that aren't needed, issues with our mindset, thinking and aspirations, or even a slowing of your progress due to frustration. So leave your past where it is and move into your future a whole lot lighter and ready to take on your world. If there are things that you realise you need to work on from your past, work on them and move on.

When it comes to moving forward, we all need to be aware which issues are ours and which are other people's. All you are in charge and in control of is your own life. Sure, there may be times when someone else's issues will cross over into your life, but essentially you need to focus on your own journey. People often tend to stick their heads in the sand hoping their problems will go away if they ignore them for long enough. But all that's good for is making things worse.

The other day I was listening to a radio interview with someone who had racked up a whole heap of personal debt. In total it was over $180 000! Not only had they maxed out one credit card, they actually managed to max out eight. At first I started to feel for the person, thinking they obviously had a limited knowledge of financial matters. But when I heard them say that it 'wasn't their fault' I changed my opinion of their situation.

This person's theory was that they shouldn't have to pay the money back because it was the banks' fault for letting them have the credit cards in the first place. They were trying to shift the blame away from themselves and on to someone else. While I think that some banks do give credit away too easily these days, the banks weren't the ones using the cards on a daily basis.

Later that day I received a phone call from someone who wanted my advice. They really wanted to buy a home but numerous banks had knocked them back due to their poor savings history. They proceeded to tell me that this wasn't fair and asked 'How come other people seem to get ahead?' What they didn't stop to consider was that those 'others' they were referring to may have put in the hard work and sacrifice, and focused themselves on reaching their financial goals. This person was focusing on others instead of themself and their own actions, or lack thereof. Like it or not, we all have to take responsibility for our actions. Sure, some things may not work out the way you had hoped or planned, and some things may really blow out in the wrong direction due to your poor decisions, but in the end the fact is we are all responsible for ourselves, our actions and all that we do, think and say.

While it may be simpler and easier to always shift the focus onto other people, why don't you stop looking for others to blame for a minute and turn your attention towards yourself and those thoughts, attitudes or actions that may have led you to the situation. Both of the people I mentioned above had the same problem: their own actions led them to the place they were in. One of them seemed to think others should take the blame and get them out of a problem they had in fact caused for themselves, whereas the other one seemed to think that he was owed something that other people had to work hard to get. They both wanted to take a short cut. Had they both removed some of their negative thinking to their own personal recycle bin and then deleted it entirely from their lives, who knows, maybe they would be in a better position right now.

Shifting blame does nothing other than prolong the inevitable—the problem is still there and will need to be dealt with sooner or later! While sometimes we can try to find others to blame and can maybe even justify in our heads that we are in the right, we are all responsible for our actions. Instead of trying to pass blame why not try to fix the problem instead? The amount of effort and frustration required to shift the blame onto others would be better utilised in solving the issue.

Take, for example, the credit card scenario above. This person may have gone too far down a path to be able to salvage anything. I just hope that instead of learning ways to pass that problem on to other people, they have learnt a more important lesson, which is how not to get into that position again.

If we don't learn anything from our mistakes, not only will we always keep making them, but the outcomes of those mistakes will eventually have bigger effects that will only cause greater misery in the future.

Empty your recycle bin every now and then

There is a little test that I would like you to do right now. For me, this is my own test to see whether I am on track with my life, my dreams and my desired results. Simply put, if you look at where you are in your life right now and make a self-assessment as to whether you are reaching the goals you have set for yourself, or you can see that you are making the right moves at least, then you will be able to make an assessment as to whether you are on track or not.

You see, the right way towards success is the way that is working, and the wrong way is the way that isn't. Simple stuff, but very true! Too many people repeatedly go down the same paths in their lives, doing the exact same thing that has never worked for them, hoping that one day it will magically work and everything they have always wanted will appear in front of their faces. This is not the right way at all. So reflect for a minute on whether you are constantly doing the same thing that isn't working. If you are, try a different approach for a while and see if you get a different and better result. In reality, we all need to understand what is important and what isn't. Often we spend time doing things that are not important at all.

These days we all seem to be running around

in a fluster, never seeming to have enough time in the day to complete what we need to get done. It seems as though once we start something that is really important and really urgent, something else pops its head up which we feel is just as important. This leads us to try to do everything at the same time, ultimately eventuating in having half-completed tasks all over the place.

This seems to occur not only with managing our time, but also when it comes to making a decision on important matters. We can sometimes rush in with an answer or solution that isn't the right one, all because we want to solve a problem as quickly as we can. So how can you manage your time correctly and how can you make sure you are making wise choices? Well, the answer is really a simple one. So simple that most people overlook it, assuming that there needs to be a deeper or harder solution. We have already discussed applying a level of importance to your decisions, and with that goes the need to apply 'the level of influence' in regards to managing your time.

Every decision that you make will influence some other part (big or small) of your life. That is why, when managing your time, you need to ensure that what you are spending your time on is influencing the rest of your life in a positive way and not adding more dramas to it. Haphazard decisions can result in outcomes that cause further or prolonged pain in your life. From today on, ensure that your time is well spent on things that help you work towards your desired outcomes. Understand that you can influence your future results today by being wise with your time and with any decisions you may need to make.

We all have the same amount of time every day and that is why you need to ensure you are capitalising on every bit of it and not wasting it on stuff that is old and useless to you. If your recycle bin is full to overflowing with stuff that has been in there for years and is not essential to your day-to-day journey, press that delete button and remove it from your life once and for all. Make more room for the things that are important and which will actually aid you in your journey.

>7

HOW TO MOVE ON AND PAST THOSE FLEAS

As you have read so far, we all have little problems or fleas that can cause major disruptions in our lives unless addressed. That is why, instead of *only* working on the major issues (the elephants), we need to look for those small things that when left alone can create a huge problem over time. Now, don't get me wrong, the big things still need to be worked on, but in one way they are easier to work on than the fleas due to them being right in your face. As you will read in this chapter, sometimes getting further ahead in life may mean changing the way you are doing things. Success in any area of your life will come when you overcome the issues that are blocking that success. If you end up stagnating you won't be useful to anyone, especially yourself.

Forget the elephants, watch out for the fleas

You need to put everything into perspective. Acknowledging the realistic size of your issues is the real key. A lot of people make their small issues quite big, instead of treating them for what they are and easily overcoming them. To be honest, I too have made little issues bigger than they were and ended up spending a lot more time on something that really didn't need the amount of effort I put in.

We all, at some time in our lives, will get to a point and wonder why it is we aren't making progress or why it is we seem to be going backwards. Sure, it may seem as though we are doing all the right things—we are busy, we are constantly moving and we even have the right feedback from people—but still nothing seems to be falling into place. If you are ever in a situation where things don't seem to be going the way you had hoped then it is okay to stop and try a different approach. There is a lot of pressure on people to succeed these days. So much so that they think that giving up and heading in a different direction is a bad thing. I don't agree with that type of thinking at all, as I never assume that everything I try will actually work out the way I think it will.

The pressure on people having to succeed at everything they do is enormous and, to be honest,

How to move on and past those fleas

at times very unrealistic. The one true fact is that not everything is going to work out the way you plan or hope for. If success was easy then everyone would be successful, so you need to realise that at some point you may not achieve what you originally set out to. As well as preparing yourself for the successes in life, you also need to prepare yourself for the disappointments that may occur in your pursuit of the success you desire.

Now before you think that I am changing my tune with regards to aiming for success, please let me explain. As you need to be deliberate with planning your success and the direction and process needed to reach it, so you should also be deliberate about when you need to give it up and stop pursuing something that just isn't going to happen the way you had planned or, more importantly, hoped for. I realise this may not sound all that motivating for you right now, but you need to learn to be a strategic quitter sometimes.

What is strategic quitting you ask? Simply put, too many people think that success is all about pushing and pushing and struggling until a result is reached. Once again, I do not agree with that at all. Some people also think there are only one or two ways for them to achieve their desired outcomes. From my perspective, success is all about knowing when to pursue something and when to walk away. The reason many people end up frustrated with aiming for levels of success in their lives is due to not knowing when to quit.

Quitting has always been seen as the easy way out and, to be honest, I believe that some people actually do quit too early without really attempting to overcome any obstacles, but I am not talking about those people here. I am talking about the people who, no matter what the circumstances, keep going and going, wishing and hoping that something will work out when in reality they are wasting their time. This is where we all need to be honest with ourselves and assess our attempts, situations and desires from a very real perspective. Why torture yourself when you could stop what you are doing and the way you are doing it and head in a totally different direction that may produce a better result? If only we all understood that there are many different ways to achieve what we desire. Your only task is to make sure that if one way doesn't work for you that you try a different one. There are many doors we can open in life, so don't think that your choices are limited. As far as I am concerned, success is a whole lot of failures put

How to move on and past those fleas

together to reach something that we have never achieved before.

I think that, within our culture, we tend to think that quitting is the easy way out—a loser's option. As stated before, I do believe some people quit too early, but there may be times when you need to suck it up and admit that things aren't going to work out and that it is time to quit. Now the process doesn't stop there. You then have to get back up on that horse and try something else in a different way this time. Don't think that you haven't progressed either; you have just found a way that didn't work, which hopefully will ensure that you don't make the same mistake again.

Success is all about reaching whatever we want to reach. There isn't a bigger prize for the person who finishes first. How long it takes is irrelevant, to be honest. Taking longer than anticipated to reach your goal is far better than not reaching it at all. That is why, to get to the next level of your life, you may sometimes need to approach reaching your goal in a totally different manner than previously attempted.

There are probably many four-letter words that come out of our mouths when things get tough or when things just don't work out for us the way we had hoped. I want to let you know what my favourite four-letter word is when I am in that situation. Before you shut your eyes expecting something bad, please read on. My favourite four-letter word is: NEXT!

That's right, when things aren't working out the way I thought they would, I just say to myself 'NEXT' and I move on. I don't dwell on it too much; I don't try to breathe life into something that is not really going anywhere. Sometimes, although it may sting, we need to be honest with ourselves and accept that some things just won't work out the way we had hoped.

I believe that too many people concentrate their energy on things that aren't going to change, and if they did change they would only change for the worst. All they end up doing is spending (or wasting) a lot of energy trying to flog a dead horse. What we all need to have is a mental trigger that says to us, 'NEXT' when we need to move on.

Each week I sit down with many people one-on-one who are after advice on starting a business, running an existing business or trying to get their personal lives back in line with their personal desires. I am constantly amazed by the amount of people who sit there and explain to me how long they have been working on something that is clearly (to them and me) not going to work out the way they thought it would. Many of those people feel that if they give up on that dream it would mean that they have failed. But I don't think that is the case at all. Just because something doesn't work it doesn't mean that it is all over, it just means that you need to either try it a different way or stop and give something else a try. Wasting energy on things that provide no results is exactly that; wasted energy that you will never get back.

There are many things I have tried that haven't worked out. Although I had success with my first business (Attitude Inc.) I was under no illusion that everything else I did from that point would work out the same way my first business did. I have started on many business ideas that ended up going the opposite way to what I imagined they would. Did I sit there for weeks or months on end trying to jump-start life into those ideas? No! I just said to myself, 'Okay, that didn't go the way I had planned. NEXT!'

Despite some failures, I still approach things with a sense of success. One of the biggest mistakes people make when things don't turn out the way they had hoped is they allow that setback to affect their attempts at anything else. So if you have suffered some disappointment or failure in the past, have a 'NEXT!' mentality and get back on the path to achieving your desires. Who knows, your greatest success may be just around the corner.

Getting caught up in the moment and trying to make something work that isn't going to will also lead to further frustration. Once you realise this you will surely be kicking yourself. I have met many people who get all excited, trying and trying to make things work that were never going to. They only end up disappointed.

Have you ever purchased something that you really couldn't afford but because you wanted it so badly you pushed yourself beyond your financial limits and signed up to a purchase plan or finance? (I did mention this in a previous chapter but it warrants another mention here.) Well, there is a bit of a process that happens in getting you to the point of purchasing and thereafter. You see, first there is buyer's excitement. You get all excited and caught up in the emotions of owning that item. But after you have bought the item you may experience buyer's regret. This is where the reality of your financial position doesn't match up with the purchase cost and the initial excitement of having something you want. While it

How to move on and past those fleas

might have seemed like a good idea at the time, you start to see why you really shouldn't have stretched yourself as much as you did. The ongoing cost of that item now outweighs the initial excitement. All of that joy and happiness is replaced with the reality of what is involved in keeping that item.

This is the same when working through some of the small issues (the fleas) in your life. Right now, at the end of this book, you may be all excited and ready to make the changes you need to make to be successful. You may get started and you may enjoy the outcomes, but after a while that initial excitement will wear off and the reality of the work involved could take the shine off what you want to achieve. This is where many people just give up. Some people believe that making positive changes to their lives will result in a state of permanent happiness. Well, I hate to be the bearer of bad news but that probably won't be the case.

Searching out all of those little things, which add up to make a huge impact on your life, will, at times, be hard work. Those of you who push through the frustration and decide right from the outset that you are prepared for the long haul will eventually be living your dreams.

The other point that needs to be made here is that you will never get to a point in your life where everything will be worked out and you will have nothing more to work on from a personal perspective. Bettering one's self is a lifelong journey. But unless you start at the beginning, which is where you are right now, you will never get to experience all that you desire. Don't rush things, though, as there is a bit of foundation work that is needed right from the get-go.

My eldest daughter has just got her learner's licence, which means two things: first, I must be getting older, and secondly, I now have something else to worry about. Jade has been waiting for this day for as long as we can remember. She was so keen to get behind the wheel and drive. So straight after she turned sixteen she went off to sit the knowledge test. I have to say the expression on her face when she got that licence in her hands was priceless, and you could feel her excitement as I drove us both home after leaving the motor registry.

Then, as I expected, Jade wanted to get straight behind the wheel. After all, she had been preparing for this day for a long time so who wouldn't want to get started straightaway? But as she got into the driver's seat, all of that excitement and anticipation came crashing down to reality. Now that she had the opportunity to finally do what she had been waiting to do, the realisation that it might be harder than first anticipated came to the forefront. Jade quickly realised that thinking how the experience would go, or imagining what it would be like, was very different to actually doing it. She had to acknowledge that driving required new skills that she didn't have yet. This was something that she needed to work on in order to achieve what she wanted. Jade then realised that she wouldn't be a fantastic and perfect driver overnight. She now understands that it will take a lot of practice and time until she can drive like she thought she would.

This is exactly the same with where we are all at in our own lives. Sure, you may have some big dreams and goals, and yes, you may have many ideas as to how things would be so much better if X, Y or Z was to happen. But even if things were to fall into place for you, you would still have to apply your learner's plate before you could master the process. It is all about taking your time instead of rushing through everything to get to the end result. Mastering skills is all about practice and commitment. It isn't about who gets there first.

Forget the elephants, watch out for the fleas

The other day Jade made a comment about how much more 'intense' driving was than she had imagined it to be. You see, all she had pictured in her head were the surface feelings of what she wanted to do and how fantastic it would be to have a licence. Whereas when you actually do the things that you had visualised for real, you have to experience the entire process, good and bad. It doesn't always work out exactly the way we pictured it. I am sure Jade thought that she could just get in the car and drive like I do. But she has to put in the hard work to learn a new skill. Most times new skills won't come naturally so we all have to work at perfecting them.

As with my daughter and her learning to drive, you too may have to be taught new ways of doing things or apply new skills to achieve your dreams. If you don't you may miss important factors or lessons, which will stop you from moving forward later on.

I am positive that if Jade doesn't understand and apply all the skills she needs to her driving throughout the learning stage, there will be no way that she will ever move past it and on to having more freedom with her car. Jade also has to complete 120 hours of all types of driving, have a logbook of these events and complete another test before she is able to go to the next level of her licence. Maybe this is a great example for us all to follow when aiming for new goals or desires. Understand that there will be a period of time before you will have the necessary skills to move forward towards your goal. Make written or mental notes as to what is working for you, or what didn't work, so that you can repeat or avoid particular methods in the future. And lastly, understand that new tasks will always require new skills as we never stop growing.

All the desire in the world will lead to nothing unless you learn to master the skills you need to turn that desire into reality. There is no reason why you cannot achieve the things that you want to achieve. The day that you understand that it probably isn't the big things that are stopping you so much as a lot of little issues that have been left to take care of themselves, is the day that you will make giant leaps towards making your desires a reality.

Don't settle for second best in your life. Put in the hard yards from today and reap those rewards. I can guarantee that you will end up kicking yourself if you don't make any changes to what you are currently doing.

Forget the elephants, watch out for the fleas

Remember: you will come across many elephants in your life that you have to overcome, but it is those pesky little fleas that you will have to look hard to find that are more likely to cause the damage if left alone.

Each of us is going through our own journey called life. Your success is entirely up to you and you alone, so start today by addressing those fleas.

ALSOBY**JUSTIN** HERALD

Books
Would you like attitude with that?
   (978 1 74175 038 6)
What are you waiting for? (978 1 74175 037 9)
It's all a matter of attitude (978 1 74114 497 0)
How to grow your business without spending a
   single cent (978 1 74114 331 7)
Prosperity on purpose (978 1 74114 794 0)
Get motivated (978 1 74114 990 6)
So you have a great idea for a business . . .
   (978 1 74175 252 6)

All available at www.justinherald.com and from www.allenandunwin.com and all good book stores.

CDs
Personal Peak Performance (4 CD series)
Principals of Prosperity (3 CD series)
How to grow your business without spending a single cent (3 CD Series)
The 5 senses of an entrepreneur (3 CD series)
The Ultimate Business Success Series (7 CD series)
For the Young Network Marketing Entrepreneur

DVDs
Impossible is possible
The psychology of success

All available from www.justinherald.com

Let Justin help you take your idea and turn it into the business of your dreams

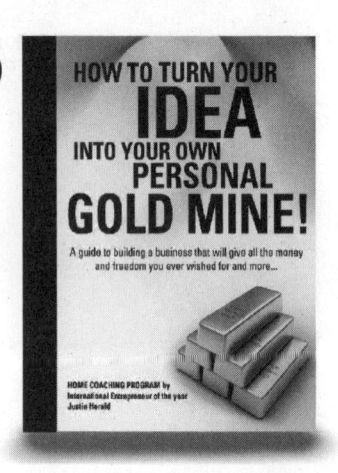

HOW TO TURN YOUR IDEA INTO YOUR OWN PERSONAL GOLD MINE!
A guide to building a business that will give all the money and freedom you ever wished for and more...

HOME COACHING PROGRAM by
International Entrepreneur of the year
Justin Herald

11 week online study course including workbook downloads and mp3 audio plu syou also get weekly email contact with Justin Herald to answer questions on the topic you are studying.

Topics include:
- It all starts with an idea
- Finding out if your idea has multi million dollar potential
- Have you got what it takes
- What you will get and what you will give
- Avoiding common mistakes
- How to develop a brand and marketing campaign that will set the world on fire
- It's all about you
- So, now you can start
- 5 Senses of an entrepreneur (3 weeks)

FIND OUT MORE ABOUT THIS PRODUCT ON JUSTINHERALD.COM

YOU DESERVE TO LIVE A RICH FULFILLING LIFE...

JUSTIN HERALD'S RICH LIFE
HOME COACHING PROGRAM

Learn the secret to lasting success and how to create massive wealth that few will ever achieve

BRAND NEW 12 CD SERIES

PRINCIPLES, LAWS & PROVEN STRATEGIES TO ACHIEVE THE LIFE OF YOUR DREAMS

Have you ever wondered why you haven't reached your goals. Do they constantly elude you no matter what you do? Then this breakthrough home coaching program will assist you in unlocking your hidden potential and enable you to live the life of your dreams.

Justin Herald has spent the last 6 years using his own success to inspire others to achieve more than they thought possible. Now after studying his own success and that of his students he has identified the key areas that you need to focus on to ensure you achieve a RICH LIFE!

This home coaching program gives you the opportunity that up until now was only available to a select few; to listen to and learn from one of Australia's most respected authorities on the subject of personal success and financial freedom.

FIND OUT MORE ABOUT RICH LIFE ON JUSTINHERALD.COM

Looking for more inspiration?

Justinherald.com is justin's official website. On here you will find all his training programs, information about upcoming events and special VIP offers. Join today to keep up to date and make the most of your journey to success.

Justin also has limited appointments each year to work with people one on one, find out more on the website about Mentoring Program.

VISIT JUSTINHERALD.COM TO FIND OUT MORE